Fig

This is a work
organizations, and events portrayed in this novel either
are products of the author's imagination or are used
fictitiously. Any resemblance to actual persons, living
or dead is purely coincidental.

© 2018 Tia Deas Norfolk VA

Dedication

Probably the hardest part of the book for me. I dedicate this book to the person that broke my heart to save HER own: myself.

Foreword

To the author,

Few people in this world will present themselves with transparency, even fewer people will give you the harsh truth about yourself in a time when you're looking for kind words but need that tough love. Tia Deas, you have the ability to present yourself, flaws and all, and accept others just as they are. Your words have always been a crutch for me when I was low and your actions have taught me to stand on my own. You are the true definition of resilient and I thank you for the ways you have touched my life and how you have helped me grow. You have always been there for me through heartbreaks and growing pains and in return I have tried to give you the love you needed instead of the love you were seeking. My sister, I am proud of you for jumping. Thank you for having the faith to share your truths with the world, in hopes of helping someone else work through their issues. This book is a testament to your strength, this book is your healing, and this book is your growth. You DESERVE this moment and I love you!

To the reader,

This book is raw and necessary for whatever you may be going through. Use it to help you heal, use the lessons to guide you to your own definition of self-love and then pass this book on. The world needs more love and it starts within you! I am proud of you for taking this jump with Tia and facing your truths head on. The best way to get the love you deserve is to start by learning from the love you once lost. Be grateful to those who hurt you and made you feel low because they provided you with the keys that will lead you to your own happiness. This journey will be a process but, in the end, I hope you are able to look yourself in the mirror and smile for the strength and the insight this book will give to you. I believe love conquers all and you should love with a fierce heart, just make sure you share that love with yourself above anyone else. Have the strength to choose you when things seem bad and keep looking at the world with positive eyes. I wish you the best on this journey...

Love,

Kala Funderburk

Acknowledgement

First, I would like to thank my Lord and Savior who loves me more than I love myself and pushes me pass limits I set for myself. I would like to thank my family for their support in my life, but especially my father for his constant support and motivation throughout this writing process. I have to thank Tristan for being the beautiful child that strengthens and motivates me daily. As a teacher, I am motivated and strengthened by my students so shout out to Norview Middle.

I have the best circle of girlfriends in the world, so here's the list of acknowledgements just for you Ladies: Laurence Pierre-Louis aka LP, Rhavin, Rika, KellyAnn, Tayleur, Bre, Ruth, Tracy, Keesh, Naomi, Chelle, Ashley, Natalie, Adama, Jasmine, Breannah, Shaqona, and many more. Love y'all from the bottom of my heart. I have the best circle of men in the world, so here is the list of acknowledgements just for you Good men: Melvin Deas and Tristan Deas, my rocks, Christopher Spriggs, C. Antwan Bynum, Duffy, Dylan, Everett, Julian, Rasheed, Rick, Jarret, DJ Izzy, Malcolm, Matt O., Malachi, Rob Hill for inspiration, and many many exes that blessed me with lessons.

My support system was just awesome: my mentor Sonya Russell, my department head Andrea Taylor, RIH my assistant principal LaDawn Durant, my strength at school Ms. Peele, my hands-on manager Kala Funderbunk, my awesome representation in Chiara Shelton, my assistance in publishing Fanita Moon Pendleton of Urban Moon Books and many many people who believed in me from jump.

You are appreciated! Thank you!

Connect with Tia

Email: figurativekeys@gmail.com

Twitter: @figurativekeys

IG: @figurative_keys

Facebook: Figurative Keys

Website: www.figurativekeys.com

Figurative Keys to Locked Doors

Tia Deas

Contentment Is On My Face

Jumping right into it, I have always been okay as LONG as I have someone, and I mean anyone, by my side. This meant I didn't have to deal with myself. I would often shift my personal problems to make them problematic issues for whomever I was with. For a while, it was good. No one could tell that I was going through simply because my eyes could not tell what my mind and body would not accept. Everything that you experience in life is not an us problem, sometimes; most times the problem is a you problem and you have to be content enough to move out of the us section of your life to a you section to work them things out. It's easier said than done because people often make themselves convenient to your calls and texts when you should cope alone. It's necessary though to be able to grow into the person you need to be for YOURSELF and anyone else. Grab a pencil or a pen! This is an interactive book, meaning while I'm working through some things, you have to work through them too. Turn the page and let's start wiping the contentment off our faces.

Contentment Barriers...

There are people and things that allow us to not grow to our potential because they accept inadequate or incomplete parts of us that could be completed if we were to work through them alone. Take at LEAST five minutes and list seven to nine contentment barriers that you use OFTEN to not deal with yourself or your problems...

1.

2.

3.

4.

5.

6.

7.

8.

9.

Just Fine For Now

If only she could stop defending this toxic cycle of he will eventually get it right.

She stays because she knows that if she does right by him, he will do right by me.

When things don't occur that way, her excuse of the pros outweigh the cons gets old

And then the excuses of maybe he wasn't taught right starts to flow.

From her mouth and her hands, turn pages to books to assess the situation of maybe he's dealing with depression

From lessons he should have learned as a boy.

Before he became a man and had to learn to defend and protect not only himself but the woman that became attached to the hip and tries to take a stab at being everything he lacked in childhood.

Pondering over missed opportunities of him making it in the league and receiving that positive affirmation he needed from everyone else but himself.

So she cannot pass go and take shelter in his heart

Because the things he lacks in internal comprehension is tearing him apart

Instead of building him up, she's breaking him down with constant obligations and angry dissertations of how he has yet to become a man and understand that what he gives he will ultimately get back.

Frightening part to her is he couldn't see that

What he lacked in power he made up in courage and though he's not perfect, he's indestructible if he can just see that excuses for what he lacks or the ones that she gives for him are unnecessary.

If only she could stop defending this toxic cycle of eventually he will figure it out

But she wanted to become his rib so these excuses keep flowing out her mouth.

Convenience

When I got to act like my feelings don't outweigh this vibe that I can't deny between us because of the bad blood that exists and persists because you decided to be less than what you promised...

I get mad, but I stay in place and take what I can get because I've become sick and tired of men leaving and you always stay...

It's time to self-reflect. This is the only thing I need you to do along the way so you can mature in this process with me. Reflection DOES NOT mean beating up on yourself, but it does require you to acknowledge what has happened and grow from it. Reflect on your own contentment barriers. How can you escape them going forward?

In A State Of Disbelief

By now, you have a little sense of my personality. I am very hopeful in people and give people the benefit of the doubt to come into my life with this open-door policy. I usually have no guards at my gate and that has not always made for the best outcome. Not everyone that comes into your life is there for your good or your growth. Some come to take what they see in you because they lack it within themselves. We have to be careful who we let in and how they are occupying our space and time. Especially those that come in saying they only want to help you or heal you. These are the people that have left me in the state of disbelief. It's because I believed in people so much, I stopped protecting myself and the very people who said they came to help or heal left me HURT.

Now what I want you to do in this moment is be vulnerable with yourself. Not with me, not with your significant other or spouse, but yourself. There are people in our lives that have shown signs that they DO NOT have good intentions for our lives and we have ignored them time after time giving them passes to treat us less than what we deserve. So now in this moment, write down some names of some people that have shown you they do not value the relationship you all possess. I'm not saying burn the bridge; I'm just asking you take a step back, look over the names and figure out how you could walk differently across the bridge or maybe even AROUND it.

1.

2.

3.

4.

5.

6.

7.

8.

9.

Spared Feelings

I wonder has he even thought about me since I left…

Does the thought of me still make him smile…

Am I still that thing that keeps him going at work…

Or was I ever more than just a pretty face and a tight ass…

Never let emotions drive you too far off track, I know exactly what they mean by that now

A kiss is like opening up the world to your heart

Things all of a sudden get kinda personal. Feelings get stronger; rationale gets weaker

And you end up saying I love you before you really knew what was transpiring

He says it first so you feel that the time is right.

You should say it back; mean it; I love you too

Now you opened your heart; for what is to come; no one really knows; but they try to warn you.

They say he shouldn't be taken seriously; like he's a game or something you know…

But my heart was already too deep, too lost… too far gone.

There were signs, but I ignored them

Said he's the man for me, it'll work out I know it will cuz by then…

My emotions lived on his every word, people became a blur, their words like music to a deaf ear

Their actions like motion to the blind; unnoticed but sensed.

Pushing past angry words through my thrown phone, I realize what the thought of being loved did to me

I see him in different eyes now that my senses are back and my heart is rationalizing the situation

It wasn't love that drove us where we went

It was the thought we could let ourselves go in the end for each other

But we lost the map and lost on two different streets…

But still as I think back over our relations and good times shared…

I wonder has he even thought about me since I left

Does the thought of me still make him smile?

Am I still that thing that keeps him going at work?

Or was I ever more than a road taken by the mind to avoid the heart and spare the feelings felt…

Self-Reflection time, yes, it is here again. Take a moment to yourself and write down some thoughts that come to mind. Think about the unbelievable moments with the people in your life and past relationships. It's better to let it out than to hold it in.

When You Think They Need You

My heart has always been a little heavy. I have the tendency to care TOO much about what others need from me and NOT enough about what I need to do and be for myself. The process of learning to let others actually want you, but NOT have you is one I've yet to acquire because I wish to help and impact as much as possible. I can be honest; I hate having to tell anyone no especially if I feel like they NEED me. But the honesty in life is you need yourself more than anyone else needs you. And if you don't come to the rescue, trust, they will still get things done. We must stop making ourselves so AVAILABLE to be used. Because NOT everyone needs a good heart or spirit to take or break.

Are you necessary?

Think back over the last few weeks or months in your life in which you have heard someone say they needed you or your services. Did they really? Or was it convenience? Was it obligation? Was it the simple fact that they knew you wouldn't say no? List (honestly, I had to say this part) the last 3-5 times you were really needed, why, and could you have said no... then tell me if they could have received the same outcome WITHOUT you...

1. Who was it:

    a. Did they need you?

    b. What did they need from you?

    c. Was it convenient or did they really need you?

    d. Was it obligation or you didn't say no?

    e. Could they have done it without you?

2. Who was it:

    f. Did they need you?

    g. What did they need from you?

    h. Was it convenient or did they really need you?

    i. Was it obligation or you didn't say no?

    j. Could they have done it without you?

3. Who was it:

    k. Did they need you?

    l. What did they need from you?

    m. Was it convenient or did they really need you?

    n. Was it obligation or you didn't say no?

    o. Could they have done it without you?

4. Who was it:

   p. Did they need you?

   q. What did they need from you?

   r. Was it convenient or did they really need you?

   s. Was it obligation or you didn't say no?

   t. Could they have done it without you?

5. Who was it:

   u. Did they need you?

   v. What did they need from you?

   w. Was it convenient or did they really need you?

   x. Was it obligation or you didn't say no?

   y. Could they have done it without you?

Tall Walls and Closed Hearts

His personality, like a fire to the fireplace I have made up in my mind that keeps me warm during lonely cold nights...

Our chemistry killed the poisons and germs of our past marked by angry pathogens that only wanted to attack the good in our souls....

I met him in a state of dead, walking blindly through a course of I love you with raised hands, balled fist, and unforgiving sorry I hurt you's...

But I figured the Hell with him was better than the Hell in myself trying to figure out how Heaven got so far away...

His body, another fence that led to a castle of walls and hearts closed due to trespassing and unexpected guest...

So, to become free to be a spirit that guided over the walls built and the locked hearts, I forgot about the common sense that guided any and all decisions...

The walls then became words and warm bodies lying together to keep pain out for each other until the guard fell weak with lies and deceit of want for more...

Storms rumbling outside the gate broke the first wall down and the enemy of angry words, past references to a life lived, and unhappiness plunged in head first...

Causing the closed heart to harden and grow sealed with soot from the destruction of a foolproof wall of you weren't supposed to be like everyone else...

So then, the souls sink into a place of maybe the walls were never meant to keep us in…just to keep the feelings that came with acknowledgement out…

And for some reason, they can no longer… be found…

Decoded

I just don't understand how you expect me to be everything you're not.

How you criticize the encrypted flaws of my existence because you aint shit, yet you expect me to be a comfort at your side when your life is low and poison to the public, if they dare take arms against your journey to manhood.

It can be understood and expected for me to support if I had a shield to protect; but instead I have a mirror for you to reflect on the fact that I'm intact and in control of the other thing I know: myself.

I know who and how I am because I decided I can't live for them, they and you; but, back to you and the indifferences you feel because I actually give you real answers and solutions to problems you face.

A taste of your own medicine in unanswered calls and texts, long exaggerated verses of why I can't make this or that instead of the truth, or even hate because you didn't do what I wanted you to.

I decided to be your reflection of the neglect you gave to the pursuit of ship, not acknowledging the lack of relations and separation in between.

I just don't understand how you expect me to be everything you're not.

How you criticize the encrypted flaws within yourself but turn around and tell me I aint shit.

Self-reflection time: It is okay to feel obligated to people if they have meaning or depth in your face, but make sure you realize what all you are giving out to others that you might need. You cannot continue to pour into others and leave your own cup empty. Take a moment or two and self-reflect on the things and people you have made your time and yourself obligated to. Is it or are they worth it?

When You Want Them To Want You

I believe it's natural to be wanted. I cannot tell you the length I have gone to be seen, wanted, or desired by someone that was absolutely NO GOOD for me. But you live and learn and in turn learn to really live. The thing with me wanting people to want me, I sometimes forgot to want the best for myself. I knew what I needed, but I was so focused on being wanted that I did not tend to myself, as I should have. I suffered from the want of others because I lacked want of myself. It took some soul searching to be honest with myself and see that what I wanted in other people wanting me, were things I already had if I focused on myself.

Is it Really Worth it? Having someone want you sometimes comes at an expensive price. If wanting them to want you means losing what you need for you, did you really come out on top? Think over the past few relations you desired. Ponder over what they wanted from you and what you ultimately needed. Would it work out for your good?

Who was it?

What did they want from you?

What did you need from yourself?

Would it have worked out for your good having them?

Who was it?

What did they want from you?

What did you need from yourself?

Would it have worked out for your good having them?

Who was it?

What did they want from you?

What did you need from yourself?

Would it have worked out for your good having them?

Left on Read

There were never really any expectations...

Take that back, maybe a few...

Here and there, you don't have to call, scattered around, no text back today...

Adjustment occurred in the mind when the body could no longer conform to the lines of lies that kept me warm in my bed waiting on your breath to coexist with mine...

Separation prolonged my skin from turning into pricks to spike anyone that came close enough to understand the pain that existed from the lack of want...

Denial took place before the feet stopped walking to the phone that lay on the bed because I already knew it wasn't even you...

Laughter erupted from my soul as I let go of the expectation that you somehow cared about the baring of my heart to your protected castle of thoughts and reasoning...

Sadness, the purest form, came after with waterfalls and physical aches that crept into the lonely night with me...

The abandonment discouraged me from attempting to call you back, embracing only sentiments of I wasn't good enough, accepting solitude as punishment for double texting when I was already Left on Read...

But there were never really any expectations…

I take that back, just a few…

I expected my mind to care enough about my heart so I would not pick up the phone and call you…

Again…with the expectation you would actually pick up

Floors

Knee deep in his shit, I scrub until the surface reflects
only who I desire to be
In the bright lights, it's an illuminated version of myself
I've yet to meet.
Free of fault, the scrubbing made me see someone that
I'm not yet to be
But still time hasn't taught me how to adjust because that
image I see is me.
Knee deep in his shit, I polish until the surface reflects
only who I desire to be
In the dimming lights, it's a shifting version of myself
I've yet to meet.
Free of frustration, the polishing made me see someone
I've been yearning to be
But still time hasn't taught me how to accept it because
that image is me.
Knee deep in his shit, I stand until the surface reflects
only what I desire it to be
In the dark, there is nothing to see but the shining parts of
me
Free to focus on the inadequate parts of what I've been
trying to be...
Because time taught me everything I think I am, despite
him, I will be.

Reflection time! Take a moment or two to reflect on the times when you desired to be wanted and slighted yourself of your own worth to have someone around. Do not bash yourself; just be honest and praise yourself in the growth you have made!

Finding Your Fucking Self...

I'm going to be honest. This chapter took me a while to get right because I hated facing the reality that I needed to be ALONE and get myself together. So easily, I can become consumed in someone else's praise or admiration of me that I forget who I am and why I'm necessary. The lack of love within myself started at a young age and only grew worse from the deflection that I gave to it. These poems are personal journals of me finding myself without a man to say he made me or he helped me be the awesome woman that I AM. No reflection at the end of this. Just a set of poems that define the independence that I have finally decided to show.

Just One Key Belonging to Me

You don't know the little girl that wishes her mother's love covered all the pieces and broken fragments of life that are put together in a body that has never been thick enough for the man that she once desired to love until the woman he sought after told him he wasn't good enough. So he returns knowing that his words of worship and praises of affection for her inadequate comprehension of herself would secure him a spot in the puzzle she pieced together daily to make sure she, by all standards, was wanted

You don't know the teenage girl that worships the very ground the first man to take her as she is walks on not understanding the ground is dirty and so many people have walked on or through the same passageway she walks alongside him receiving stares of confusion and cuts of eyes too blind to see she doesn't need love from anyone else other than herself. So he stays and bruises up her body mind and heart with his words of frustration, his blows of unresolved discrepancies with past people, his gifts of miscommunication that allow her to feel needed in her puzzle she pieces together daily to make sure she, by all standards, was loved

You really don't know the woman that wanted to explain to any and all souls around that no man could come in anymore and fill voids that she allowed insignificant men to occupy while she vested herself into being wanted and loved by the wrong group of pursuers claiming they were there to make her better.

So he comes back around trying to find an open door to the room of the house that's always been available for him to stay and take space when he's done playing around with the rest. But the doors were locked, the windows were closed, the leaks in the house were even patched. With a note on the door stating: I was searching for so much want and love in you but I need it from myself more. There is no spare key for this door.

Single Mother Sorry

I hope he can understand that I didn't enter into motherhood knowing what I lacked stacked behind books and pages of lessons others mothers and grandmothers of the world tried to teach young girls that decided to move forward with pregnancy regardless of the outcome of a father staying or leaving but having to raise a man. Let me start by saying sorry.

I hope he can understand that I didn't intend on giving him anything less than what he deserved in care, love, and protection but I lacked affection because the inner parts of me were still attempting to learn to love myself without affirmation from no one else and when he came I was still trying to figure out how to place what love I found in myself in his mouth so he could grow and be happy unlike me who had become a stereotype; no longer a black queen in my own eyes. I didn't see my own greatness baby, Mommy will do better.

I hope he can understand that I never wanted him to face the fear of not being good enough when my times and opportunities were too tough and I pushed him away in anger when all he wanted to do was play and make my day brighter than it was because In his world I've been his only truth to how happiness can begin and end but with me being overwhelmed trying to be everything for him I thought I lacked I overlooked that and lost the only friend I had, please forgive me.

I hope he can understand that I never intended to be both single and his mother not possessing the qualities I once had when I had the man that was his father by my side as a ride or die not riding nor dying for a cause once having a young boy to have to raise into a man and understand that he cannot be in love with anyone else until he will learn to ride the waves and die standing up, not laying down to a system of inadequacy or inefficiency, for himself. I do apologize.

I hope he can understand that I didn't enter into motherhood not understanding that all I lacked in the beginning was him and he is the only key that I needed to place into the locked door to love myself. I hope he can understand that I didn't intend to fall into love with the boy he is because I thought I lacked a man to give love to, until he looked me in my eyes and I realized that single motherhood won't be my demise. I hope he can understand that I didn't want to raise him without a man at my side but I needed him to myself for a while so I could learn to survive. By myself for US. Sorry, not sorry.

Taking Accountability

There are ALWAYS signs. They are BIG and they instruct us to detour from what we are pursuing or reaching for. Sometimes the signs come in the form of a no when you expected a yes and sometimes the sign comes in the form of a big feeling in the pit of your stomach. However they occur, we must take accountability for that knowledge when it does. As good as it looks on the other side, it might just be worse off. Knowing you are worth more than that person can handle and still giving them access to your excellence affects you and your blessings, not theirs. You must take charge of how you let people invade your space and privacy. You cannot and will not continue to let people mismanage you and your heart when you take accountability for yourself and face reality. Just because they are good to me does NOT mean they are good for me. Take that accountability for yourself.

Checks and Balances

This is a system I had to get myself into doing daily because some things don't add up in my life and when they don't, I have to make some changes. Sometimes I have to add and sometimes, I have to subtract. I want you to think of the people in your outer circle you associate with on a weekly or monthly basis. If you only have an inner circle, think of them at this point. If they are adding to your life in any way, give them 5 points. If they are taking from you in any way, subtract 5 points. If they take more than they give though, give them 3 points and take the 5 you give. See who really balances out in your life and who is draining your account...

Person #1

On a scale of 1-5, how much do they give?

On a scale of 1-5, how much do you take?

Subtract how much they give from what you take.

Does it balance out?

Person #2

On a scale of 1-5, how much do they give?

On a scale of 1-5, how much do you take?

Subtract how much they give from what you take.

Does it balance out?

Person #3

On a scale of 1-5, how much do they give?

On a scale of 1-5, how much do you take?

Subtract how much they give from what you take.

Does it balance out?

Person #4

On a scale of 1-5, how much do they give?

On a scale of 1-5, how much do you take?

Subtract how much they give from what you take.

Does it balance out?

Saying it Right

Don't make me like you on purpose

I'm not even playing hard to get

But I can't fathom to be hit by the arrow from the fellow

Who doesn't understand that I'm just a girl in a world full of men

Who have the art of writing with a pen lies and deceit to get underneath

To the things that cream and scream when he elevates his dick

In between me and my body convulses in actions unidentified

Such as can we be more than friends…

Then and only then he drops the pen because the words he once said weren't true

And her heart had now turned a virtuous color of blue.

Reflection time! After looking at the dynamics of how people can negatively and positively affect you as you give them access to you, do you feel differently about them? Are you going to change how you talk or walk with them? Are you going to hold yourself accountable for how relationships make, take away, or break you? This is why taking accountability is necessary. If you know what a person does to you and for you and it doesn't balance out, you're ONLY hurting yourself.

Stretch Marks

Why do we get stretch marks? They're VISIBLE indications of growth on our body. Now I know stretch marks are NOT always admired or lust after, but it's the body's way of letting you know you're growing and progressing into something bigger. In life, stretch marks are considered those texts you receive that you no longer feel the need to text back to or the exes that you no longer shade when you come back into contact with him or her. The habits that you used to engage in that were not the best are examined. The responses and reactions you give now to old situations are examined. Of course, step by step, day by day. But not allowing people to take you from 0-100 like you used to should be praised. The stretch mark should shout Victory! All your stretch marks should represent growth that has allowed you to be better than before. Embrace them.

Growth Indicators...

We know that growth produces those stretch marks we need for the body to grow. Compile a short list of things you know you have been able to grow in. Think about it like a praise report for yourself. You deserve it! We have been reflecting and collecting ourselves to move forward so now it is time to let these stretch marks show.

The Thing I used do:

What I do Now:

Growth Indication:

The Thing I used do:

What I do Now:

Growth Indication:

The Thing I used do:

What I do Now:

Growth Indication:

The Thing I used do:

What I do Now:

Growth Indication:

Praise report: I have grown in the following areas of my life:

AND

I'm proud of myself!

Get the Fuck Out

But I'm serious though in the most unapologetic way…

No knocks on my door but it's open and there's a stranger in my home…

You came in uninvited, wiped your dirty feet on my clean floor, and didn't even concern yourself enough to close my door…

I could not see myself kicking you out without having even welcomed you in…

Washed your feet using only what steps you took to find me… but forgot to ask you what direction you see yourself going with or without me…

Gave you some socks to protect your scars of abandonment, the cuts of confusion, the calluses of mismanagement from others…

Lotioned the fears of tomorrow with hopes and dreams of peace and contentment in a home built and meant for you and possibly me…

But then I have to give you some shoes so you could walk out the very door you came in… still open…

Sigh.

Hopefully I fixed with care what your ex couldn't with those torn bandages of heartache… and love you the way I shouldn't to make the wounds heal…

So my get the fuck out won't hurt you like the footprints you left in my heart, I mean home do… as I'm closing my door.

Leaving Those Uninvited Behind

Can you believe it? We have made it to the end of a journey of self-love; we only have a few selections, and one more reflection left. It is crazy that in writing this book, I was able to really spotlight my own experiences and ask myself why I have not taken my own advice. It is so easy to see the flaws in what others do, but self-reflection will do some things to your soul if you let it. The purpose of self-love is to grow and be complete in yourself so you are not out here attempting to find someone to complete you. Been there, done that! Lol. It is time to find someone who compliments your complexity. And leave those other people, whether they be in the past or the present, behind. Not everyone deserves access to the greatness you possess.

VIP

Can't believe we have finally made it to the big leagues of figuring out who is important and who is uninvited to the show we have to perform. Oftentimes, those people who have front row seats still don't understand all you have to offer or the beauty of your gifts. But if they show they deserve to have a seat in your life or at your table, give them VIP. Show those who truly care they are important as long as you love and treat yourself first! Last activity would be to create your own table with you at the head and place those people who deserve to be in the VIP around you. Get creative if need be and put a gate around the table for those that CAN'T get in.

Castle Walls

Can you imagine a world, a utopia, matter of fact

Where love was first, family was second, and dreams came last

Where there were no broken hearts or tattered wings

She was happy, so was he; meaning they were living the life

I saw that life once, yes, my eyes were wide open

Love, spiritually and emotionally propelled them into their own kingdom

With knights and lords, a big castle with a moat

Day after day love grew within them;

Not only for each other but for the connection they shared

Outside world set aside; knights won't let them in

Guarding day and night; no militia able to break down the walls

That strength, that power, that lust in each other to satisfy their partner's soul

That was me and you…In a far distant land and time…

Hearts divinely selected together, minds on that same comprehension level

Meaning I understand you, and you understand me

But all good stories must close chapter and start a new book

The book now banished in all lands near and far

This community don't accept love; change; happy people

When you say I'm sorry I hear people saying you don't mean it

How would they know and why do they care?

Have we become so tied up in the skepticism of society

We don't know where loves comes from

What it can and will do for me and you cuz if you did, I'll remind you

Hung on a cross; crucified for his people; just to rise again and say: I love you

Man, I just want to go back to that utopia, be with them people, see what they see

But in the end, I understand that the change truly starts within me…

So ima love hard, and ima love all; and hope my castle walls will never fail or fall…

He Left Marks over Me

Not look him up and down, not take in the goodness

Of his smell, his tact, his taste because it's designed to blind the very eyes

That unlock my soul and tell me it's okay to be with you

In private, but not in public because it would be the topic or subject of everyone

Outside those four walls that you convinced me mattered the most

During a storm or test that we take in life because those results promote

Staying together even if it gets dark outside and you leave me alone again.

Not look him in his face, not take up his case,

not falter under pressure because he is NOT my man and

make myself understand that he did not protect me.

Instead he deflected his insecurities and inadequacies on me

telling me to change in trying situations of whether or not

I should come alongside him in a storm with no raincoat or hat

and get wet and sick of all the bullshit he calls caring for me.

Not look him in the eyes, not believe his lines

Of recycled promises of honesty that would promote a harmony

Which would subject me to understand that what he lacked as a man

He found in me making me the very woman he wanted but couldn't handle

Because he believed the label of handle with care meant I was fragile,

When in actuality the ticking time bomb in me started off the countdown

To boot his obnoxious way of learning to love himself out

I'm borderline I love him/fuck this nigga...

I can't subject myself to a man that doesn't understand I've been THE clout.

Reflection, Reflection, Reflection… this time around, it's going to be a little different. Tell yourself nothing but POSITIVE affirmations about how you plan and will move forward at this point. I believe in you and glad you took this time to glow up with me.

Afterword

First, from the bottom of my heart, thank you for reading and traveling with me on this journey to understanding yourself through my eyes. Taking the time to read my poems and my dialogue and participate in the soul cleansing activities honestly brings tears to my eyes. I had all these dreams as a child to be a teacher, an author and a mother. Crazy how I prayed for the days I am experiencing now. I am blessed to have wonderful readers like you to bliss in these moments with me. Now, moving forward, I NEED your feedback. Tell me what you think, tell me how it made you feel, and tell me if I helped you out in any way... I live my life for impact and I want to know if the book had an impact on you! Send all messages and feedback to figurativekeys@gmail.com. I appreciate you in advance for the feedback. If you want a signed copy of the book or to meet up to talk about it, send the inquiries to the email as well. There will be book signings and public appearances to come so stay linked with me on the facebook page figurative keys and my IG @figurative_keys. Love you all. Thank you so very much!

About The Author

Tia L. Deas was born in Orangeburg, South Carolina, on July 27, 1992. She grew up in Stone Mountain, Georgia and Cocoa, Florida, before settling in Norfolk, Virginia. She is the mother to a handsome son named Tristan Deas. She received her Bachelors of Arts in English Literature in 2016. She will receive her Masters of Arts in Teaching English in December of 2018. She is currently in her second-year teaching 6th grade English for Norfolk Public Schools. Tia is a member of Zeta Phi Beta Sorority Incorporated and Order of Eastern Star. Her passion is affecting her community and the world. Tia enjoys reading, playing bingo, and traveling the world. Change is her motivation.

Tia Deas

Coming Soon

Figurative Keys to Family Matters

Figurative Keys to Toxic Cycles

Figurative Keys to Single Motherhood

95867844R00046